Contents

Any words appearing in the text in bold, **like this**, are explained in the Glossary.

 Find out more about thunder and lightning at www.heinemannexplore.co.uk

What is a thunderstorm?

A thunderstorm is a storm where we see flashes of lightning and hear claps of thunder. It brings tall dark clouds.

A thunderstorm can last for a few minutes or many hours.

Watching the Weather

Thunder and Lightning

Elizabeth Miles

www.heinemann.co.uk/library

To order:
☎ Phone 44 (0) 1865 888066
🖹 Send a fax to 44 (0) 1865 314091
🖥 Visit the Heinemann Bookshop at www.heinemann.co.uk/library to browse our catalogue and order online.

First published in Great Britain by Heinemann Library, Halley Court, Jordan Hill, Oxford OX2 8EJ, part of Harcourt Education.
Heinemann is a registered trademark of Harcourt Education Ltd.

Editorial: Nicole Irving and Tanvi Rai
Design: Richard Parker and Celia Jones
Illustrations: Jeff Edwards and Paul Bale
Picture Research: Rebecca Sodergren and Mica Brancic
Production: Séverine Ribierre

Originated by Dot Gradations Ltd.
Printed and bound in China by South China Printing Company

ISBN 0 431 19026 7
09 08 07 06 05
10 9 8 7 6 5 4 3 2 1

British Library Cataloguing in Publication Data

Miles, Elizabeth
    Thunder and Lightniing. – (Watching the Weather)
    551.5'632
A full catalogue record for this book is available from the British Library.

Acknowledgements

The Publishers would like to thank the following for permission to reproduce photographs: Corbis/Jose Luis Pelaez, Inc. p. 5; Corbis/Ray Bird p. 22; Corbis/Raymond Gehman p. 17; Corbis/RF pp. 4, 10; Corbis/Roger Ressmeyer p. 26; Corbis/Tom Bean p. 14; FLPA p. 25; Getty images/Digital Vision p. 6; Getty Images/Photodisc pp. I, 11; Getty/Image Bank p. 16; Harcourt Education Ltd/Tudor photography pp. 28, 29; Rex features/Kim Ludbrook p. 27; Science Photo Library/George Post p. 9; SPL/Munoz-Yague/Eurelios p. 18; SPL/Jim Reed pp. 20, 21; SPL/Keith Kent pp. 12, 15; SPL/Pekka Parviainen p. 8; SPL/Peter Menzel p. 19; Zefa p. 13.

Cover photograph of lightning over Tuscon, reproduced with permission of Corbis/Tom Ives.

The Publishers would like to thank Daniel Ogden for his assistance in the preparation of this book.

Every effort has been made to contact copyright holders of any material reproduced in this book. Any omissions will be rectified in subsequent printings if notice is given to the Publishers.

The paper used to print this book comes from sustainable resources.

The rain that falls during a thunderstorm can make you very wet, very quickly!

Everyone runs for cover when a thunderstorm begins. Thunderstorms often bring lots of rain and sometimes even **hail**.

What is lightning?

Lightning is a flash of light in the sky. A lightning flash can happen in less than a second. If you blink, you might miss it!

Lightning can jump from cloud to cloud.
Sometimes it jumps from a cloud to the
ground. It can also hit trees and houses.

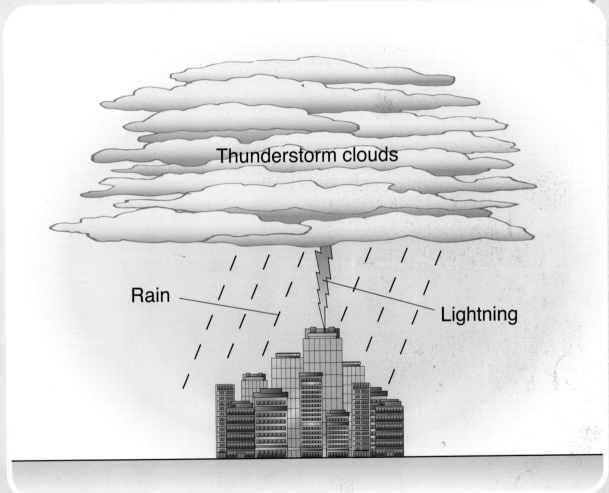

Thunderstorm clouds

Rain

Lightning

What causes lightning?

Electricity causes lightning. There is electricity in thunderstorm clouds. Sometimes this electricity causes giant sparks of hot light. These are flashes of lightning.

The electricity that causes lightning comes from tall storm clouds like this.

Lightning is very bright because it is very hot. A flash of lightning is about five times hotter than the surface of the Sun.

What is thunder?

Thunder is the noise you can hear in a thunderstorm. Lightning sparks heat the air so quickly that it **explodes**. This makes the clap of thunder.

Thunder happens at the same time as lightning, but we see the lightning before we hear the thunder. This is because light travels through air faster than sound.

Thunder can be very loud if you are close to the storm.

Lightning shapes

Lightning takes different shapes. Forked lightning splits into branches. It may come down from the cloud to the ground. It can also go across the sky to another cloud.

This forked lightning is jumping from cloud to cloud.

Sheet lightning looks like a brilliant white light.

When a lightning flash is hidden behind a cloud it is called sheet lightning. The cloud hides the lines of the flash, so we mostly see their glow.

Thunderstorms and animals

If lightning hits sheep in a field it can kill them.

Thunderstorms can be dangerous. It does not happen very often, but lightning can kill animals in fields.

Lightning can even kill fish in a lake. This is because **electricity** can spread some way through water.

Lightning can jump from clouds to a lake, like in this picture.

Lightning and plants

Lightning often strikes tall things, such as trees. It is dangerous to stand under a tree during a storm. If the tree is struck by lightning, you may get hurt too.

Lightning can set fire to a tree. If the tree is in a forest, other trees may catch fire too. In hot summers, lightning can start huge **forest fires**.

After lightning has struck, a whole forest can be badly damaged.

Flying through a storm

Some special planes fly through storm clouds. People inside take measurements to learn more about thunderstorms. Then they send this information to **weather forecasters**.

This plane is very strong. It will not be damaged if struck by lightning.

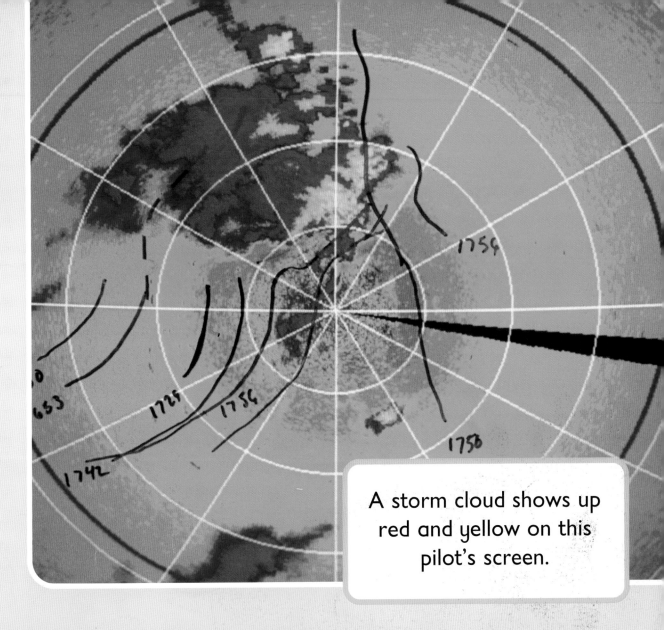

A storm cloud shows up red and yellow on this pilot's screen.

Ordinary planes have equipment that can tell if a thunderstorm is close by. If **pilots** know a storm is ahead, they can fly round it.

Storm warnings

Weather stations have lots of instruments. These measure things such as air **temperature** and wind speed.

Weather forecasters can tell us if a thunderstorm is on its way. They work out what the weather will be like by looking at different measurements.

Thunderstorms can build up on hot, sticky days. Warm air rises from the ground. If the air goes on rising very quickly, weather forecasters know a thunderstorm may form.

Dark, storm clouds cover the sky before a thunderstorm.

Staying safe – people

This tree was struck by lightning. Never stand under a tree during a thunderstorm.

Very few people are struck by lightning, but lightning can kill. In a thunderstorm, don't take any risks. You should run inside a building if you can.

Safety code

Follow these rules to be safe in a thunderstorm.

Things to do	Things not to do
• Get into a building or a car. Shut all doors and windows. • If you are in or near water, get away fast. • If there is no shelter, lie down flat on your front. • Keep away from metal or electrical things such as radiators or telephones.	• Never stand near a tree, a pole or under an umbrella. • Do not sit on a hill, run down to the bottom.

Staying safe – buildings

Lightning can damage buildings and start fires. People put **lightning conductors** on the top of tall buildings. This keeps the buildings safe.

If lightning strikes, it hits the conductor, not the building. A wire carries it down to the ground, away from the building.

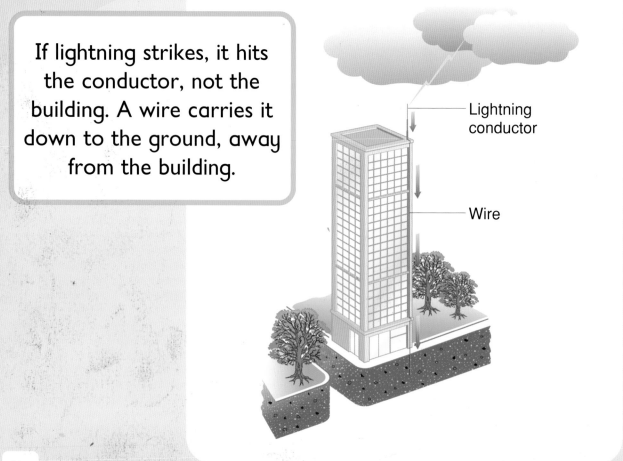

Lightning conductor

Wire

If a building is struck by lightning, things inside can be damaged. Computers, televisions and telephones should be unplugged during a thunderstorm to keep them safe.

Lightning conductors need to be placed high up on buildings to keep them safe from thunderstorms.

Disaster: lightning strikes

When lightning strikes land, it spreads like ripples in a pond. It can spread across a playing field and hurt several people at the same time.

Lightning strikes the Earth many times every day.

If lightning strikes, buildings can catch fire.

Lightning can ruin buildings and burn trees because it is hot and powerful. It heats bricks and trees so quickly that they can **explode**.

Project: making electricity

Electricity causes lightning. Try making your own electricity at home.

You will need:
• a balloon

1. Blow up the balloon and tie it at the neck.

2. Rub the balloon against your sweater or T-shirt.

3. Hold the balloon against your clothes, a wall or the ceiling. What happens? The balloon should stick.

4. You can also try rubbing the balloon against your hair.

5. Then hold the balloon a little bit away from your hair.

What happens?
Rubbing the balloon on your jumper or your hair gives it an **electrical force**. This is a little bit like the electrical force in a thunderstorm cloud. This force makes the balloon stick to your clothes. It also pulls your hair towards the balloon.

Find out more about electricity at www.heinemannexplore.co.uk

29

Glossary

electrical force force that is caused by electricity

electricity kind of energy. Many lights and machines need electricity to make them work.

explodes bursts apart

forest fires fires that burn down large areas of forest

hail pebble-shaped pieces of ice falling from clouds

lightning conductors metal rod fixed on buildings, that picks up the electricity from a lightning strike and takes it to the ground

pilot person who flies a plane

temperature measure of how hot or cold things are

weather forecaster person who works out what the weather is going to be like

weather station place where weather measurements are taken and recorded

Find out more

More books to read

Wild Weather: Thunderstorm, Catherine Chambers (Heinemann Library, 2003)

Geography Starts Here! Weather Around You, Angela Royston (Hodder Wayland, 2001)

What is Weather? Watching the Weather, Miranda Ashwell and Andy Owen (Heinemann Library, 1999)

Websites to visit

http://www.weatherwizkids.com
A website packed with information about weather features, satellite images from space, games and fun activities to do with the weather.

http://www.planetpals.com/weather.html
Learn more about different sorts of weather and interesting weather facts to share with friends.

Index

Titles in the *Watching the Weather* series include:

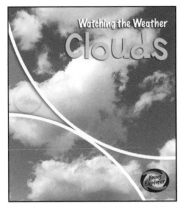

Hardback   0 431 19022 4

Hardback   0 431 19023 2

Hardback   0 431 19024 0

Hardback   0 431 19025 9

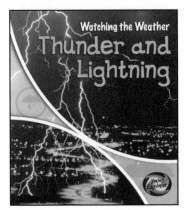

Hardback   0 431 19026 7

Find out about the other titles in this series on our website www.heinemann.co.uk/library